20 O'Carolan Irish Classics
For 5-String Banjo and All Instruments

By Tom Hanway

Online Audio

To Access the Online Audio Go To:
www.melbay.com/21599MEB

Front Cover Photo: Copper Statue of Turlough O'Carolan and Tom Hanway
Mohill, Co. Leitrim (Photo: Denise Conroy)

Online Audio Recording mastered by Jon Gordon at Jon Gordon Music Production, NYC
www.jongordon-music.com

www.melbay.com

Table of Contents

20 O'Carolan Irish Classics

Acknowledgments

I owe huge thanks to the many Gaelic and Celtic harpers who have kept the music alive across the centuries and into modern times, including Thomas Connellan (c. 1640/1645 – 1698), Robin Huw Bowen (Welsh) and Alan Stivell (Breton). I wish to recognize all the unknown musicians and steadfast composers whose music has been passed down orally and through manuscripts across centuries as a *living tradition*, and because of whom arcane collections such as mine can come to joyful fruition.

Thanks to Donal O'Sullivan (1893 - 1973), whose definitive work, *Carolan: The Life, Times and Music of an Irish Harper,* helped me to appreciate the man, how he lived, and his immense achievements as a poet and composer. O'Sullivan's own work reveals the importance of researching the origins of tunes in order to find their connections to Carolan's many patrons, and to the overlapping musical cultures of the day. The harp was still the principal musical instrument to both the Catholic and Protestant gentry of the day. Harpers were entertained as guests at the Big Houses, playing old Irish airs, taking pupils, playing weddings and funerals, and received lavish hospitality for their efforts, Turlough O'Carolan (1670 – 1738), a blind itinerant harper, poet and composer was able to prosper and gain fame in one of the most remarkable and tragic epochs of Irish history. A huge body of his music and poetry survived, while the sum total of surviving tunes by his predecessors and contemporaries numbers about thirty.

Huge thanks to Geoff Stelling for using my Celtic design ideas and specifications for the Tom Hanway SwallowTail Deluxe banjo, manufactured in both Standard and Deluxe models.

I am grateful to banjo maestro Paddy Kiernan for going over my early transcriptions and offering sound advice and playing suggestions.

Once again, I owe huge thanks to Longford's own Eddie Denniston for his technical prowess in handling the sometimes precarious data transfers. Jon Gordon at Jon Gordon Music Production, NYC, deserves special thanks for eliminating extraneous noise, especially horns, train engines and whistles in the distance, and for mixing and mastering the audio recording: www.jongordon-music.com.

I owe so much to my first mother-in-law, Aileen Low (nee Donnelly) of Perth, Western Australia, to my second mother-in-law, Mona Conroy (nee Gleeson) of Longford, Ireland, and to my beautiful parents, Elena and John Hanway II of Larchmont, New York.

This collection of classic Carolan tunes is dedicated to Kathleen Low Hanway (1960-2002), Judy Harrow (1945 –2014) and Alexei Kondratiev (1949 – 2010), cherished companions and mentors who encouraged me to learn about Celtic cultures, languages, and to play all things Celtic on the 5-string banjo.

I am thankful to the living tradition and to so many great players for accepting and encouraging the 5-string banjo at traditional sessions. Happy to Meet and Sorry to Part!

Preface

Here is a collection of Turlough O'Carolan's tunes for the 21st-century, gleaned from traditional sources while presenting clear-cut renditions of his compositions. This work stays close to the original or commonly accepted melodies while adding banjo-specific ornaments, chords, and at times, bass parts, drones and contrary motion. These settings are my own, designed specifically for 5-string-banjo – not re-hashed from Carolan collections intended for other melody instruments. I settled on these settings and fingerings by playing each tune again and again over the course of years, or even decades for certain tunes, ('Carolan's Concerto' and 'Carolan's Draught'), striving for appealing sounds and resonances, and seeking comfortable ways of laying bare or, sometimes, ornamenting the melodies.

This is my fourth Celtic tune collection with Mel Bay. It pulls together everything I have stressed all along about using one's ears, getting inside the tunes and "owning" the music. I refer the reader to the discussions in the chapters and Glossary to *Complete Book of Irish & Celtic 5-String Banjo* (1998).

My friend and mentor Bill Keith was one of the first to play tunes from that best-selling collection, and he encouraged me to transcribe Carolan's tunes for a follow-up collection. So did William A. Bay at Mel Bay Publications, Inc., and we envisaged a "Complete Book" of Carolan's music for 5-string banjo, but with well over 200 extant tunes, it seemed a daunting, quixotic task. Collin Bay (present CEO) suggested a more practical and attainable goal, and as result, I have cherry-picked Carolan's tunes specifically for Celtic fingerstyle banjo. These are fun to play, many of them deceptively simple, and they sound natural on 5-string banjo. There is no need to re-tune the instrument, and I've stuck to standard keys that players use for these tunes – keys that sound great on the banjo.

A passage I wrote in *Easy Irish and Celtic Session Tunes for 5-String Banjo: Best-Loved Jigs and Reels* bears repeating: In playing tunes at sessions across the globe, I have come to the realization that, in order to be "authentic," one needs to be creative – true to one's own muse. Surprisingly, this is especially true in "traditional" music, if the tradition is truly alive. It is a process of learning from others, taking chances, listening critically, making mistakes and learning from them, gaining a measure of confidence and mastery, and then lots of practice. There is no shame in reshaping the same piece of music over and over in the development of a composer's approach to playing: the ability to create new music and variations during a performance. Some folks like to call this "playing in the zone." It's not to be confused with "zoning out." Mastery of one's instrument is an on-going process. Finding one's own tradition (or traditions) and developing a "style" is a process of self-discovery and going back to the drawing board. Originality and authenticity are not mutually exclusive terms: One can be both innovative and traditionally-minded.

In sum, I have tried to remain faithful to Carolan's melodies while being part of the living tradition, incorporating *legato* and *staccato* techniques that work together, using harmony principles, drones, contrary motion, chords and bass lines that sound good to me, with an ear towards the Baroque era. The proof is in the pudding. I hope you have as much fun learning these tunes as I did in presenting them as springboards for serious creative endeavour. By all means, feel free to adapt these settings to suit your own tastes and musical inclinations.

Introduction

The goal of this collection is to reveal 20 timeless melodies by Turlough O'Carolan (1670-1738). Transcribed for Celtic fingerstyle banjo, I have made the tunes as straightforward as possible and included fretting and picking-hand fingerings to help students from getting their fingers all tangled up. I always indicate fingerings for both hands because I mix and match "legato" and "staccato" playing techniques in order to get the sounds I want to *hear.*

There are many possible ways of playing these tunes, for example, tending towards either a purely *legato* approach, known as *melodic, Keith-style*, or *arpa* (harp) style, or alternatively, a purely *staccato* approach, known as single-string or *Reno-style* in bluegrass. The former legato approach works beautifully for getting the steady streams of eighth-notes found in many American fiddle tunes, but tends to smooth out Celtic tunes, making them sound like *melodic-style bluegrass,* which they are not. The latter *staccato* approach works great for many styles of music, almost mimicking the sound of the tenor banjo, but because it avoids the fifth string, one is practically playing a plectrum banjo. The open sound of the 5-string banjo might be lost to overuse of single-string playing. So, in order to avoid these traps, I make technique serve the music – not the other way around – and I mix and match techniques based on how I want the tunes to *sound.* My approach to playing Celtic tunes is a very physical one, and sometimes I use a fretting-hand fingering just because I like the way it *feels*, and if it sounds right. Celtic fingerstyle techniques are used for Carolan's music, a style that has taken me over two decades to develop and master. Still, I try to avoid being a slave to technique, and I tend towards sensation and intuition in making choices about technique.

As in ***Best-Loved Jigs and Reels*** (2012) and ***Best-Loved Airs and Session Tunes*** (2013), I employ **fretting-hand techniques** (slides, hammer-ons, and pull-offs) when it feels right. **Please try to follow my fretting-hand fingerings: 1 = index, 2 = middle, 3 = ring, 4 = little finger, t = thumb.** These are written to the left and above-left of the corresponding notes in standard notation. Using the indicated fretting-hand fingerings will make things a lot easier. **Also consider my preferred picking-hand choices.** The picking-hand choices are personal preference from years of experimenting, and I find them economical and the easiest to use.

Similar to traditional bluegrass (Scruggs-style) playing, I enjoy using the thumb as much as possible, especially in places where I want to accent or emphasize a note or certain notes. I made a delightful discovery. By some extraordinary serendipity, the first half of the 'Foggy Mountain Breakdown' roll (IMTM) works perfectly for 'Carolan's Concerto', and I use it on both the outside (second and first) and inside (third and second) strings. It works comfortably for 'Carolan's Draught', 'Carolan's Ramble to Cashel', 'Henry MacDermott Roe', and many more tunes. I didn't try to put in this roll pattern: It just feels natural to use it at times.

Turlough O'Carolan – sometimes "Carolan" if just the surname is used – was an itinerant blind harper who had many patrons for whom he composed tunes with lyrics (called "planxties"). The vast majority of his verses were sung in Irish *(Gaeilge)*. For those who want to learn more about Carolan's extraordinary life and that of his many patrons through the tune histories, I recommend Donal O'Sullivan's brilliant collection, *Carolan: The Life, Times and Music of an Irish Harper.*

Those who read treble clef (G-clef) notation can also study twenty of Carolan's best-loved tunes. Those new to backing Celtic tunes, especially guitarists, can find the exact chords used on the audio recording above the standard notation. Unlike my last two collections where I kept ornamentation to a minimum, many of these tune settings embrace the Baroque, and employ arpeggios and Celtic ornaments. I found ways of getting in bass and drone notes, desired resonances and *overtones,* while avoiding unwanted resonances, *partials,* and the like. The backing tracks provide the same chords and have added some bass notes to help flesh out the tunes. Of course, there are other ways – virtually endless ways – of harmonizing these tunes.

I suggest that you work on the tunes one at a time, phrase by phrase, and take your time with them. I recommend starting with the ones that sound playable to you. Some tunes are harder than others, while some phrases within tunes take more practice than others do. Just keep going over those phrases or sections that present difficulty until the hard bits become easy. Play along with the recording to get an overall feel for a tune and to get it into your head, and then play with it yourself. Get the tune under your fingers, then go back and experiment with it some more. It's also a good idea to work with a metronome at the suggested tempos. You may want to slow down or speed up tunes later, and that's entirely up to you. Learn one tune at a time. I wish you a lifetime of fun playing these classic pieces by Turlough O'Carolan.

Tom Hanway
December 7, 2014

Tom Hanway at RTE Studios

20 O'Carolan Irish Classics For 5-String Banjo and All Instruments

♩ = 138

Welsh and Irish

Beauty in Tears

(a.k.a. Llwyn Onn / The Ash Grove)

Based on Francis O'Neill's
1903 Carolan version
Arr. Tom Hanway

Blind Mary

♪ = 120

(Máire Dhall)

Turlough O'Carolan
Arr. Tom Hanway

♩= 88

Bridget Cruise

(Third Air)

In Gratitude to
Paddy Kiernan

Turlough O'Carolan
Arr. Tom Hanway

Captain O'Kane

(The Wounded Hussar)

♩ = 132

Turlough O'Carolan
Arr. Tom Hanway

♩ = 160

Carolan's Concerto

For Kathleen Mary
Low Hanway

(Mrs. Power)

Turlough O'Carolan
Arr. Tom Hanway

D A D A G A A D A A
I T M T I M T M I M T M I M T I T I T I T M T I M T M T M I T M T I T M T I M
G D D A G G D D A A
T M T I M T M T I M T M T I T M T I M T I T I M T M I M T M I T M T M I T M I T I M I
D D Em Em D D Em A D A D D
T I T I T I T I T I M T I T M I T I M T M I T I T I T I M T M I T M M H P I M T M I T I T

Carolan's Cottage

♩ = 104

Turlough O'Carolan
Arr. Tom Hanway

Am F C Em
Am F C Am
Dm C F Em
Am Am Am E Am

♩= 128

Carolan's Draught

For Denise Conroy

Turlough O'Carolan

Arr. Tom Hanway

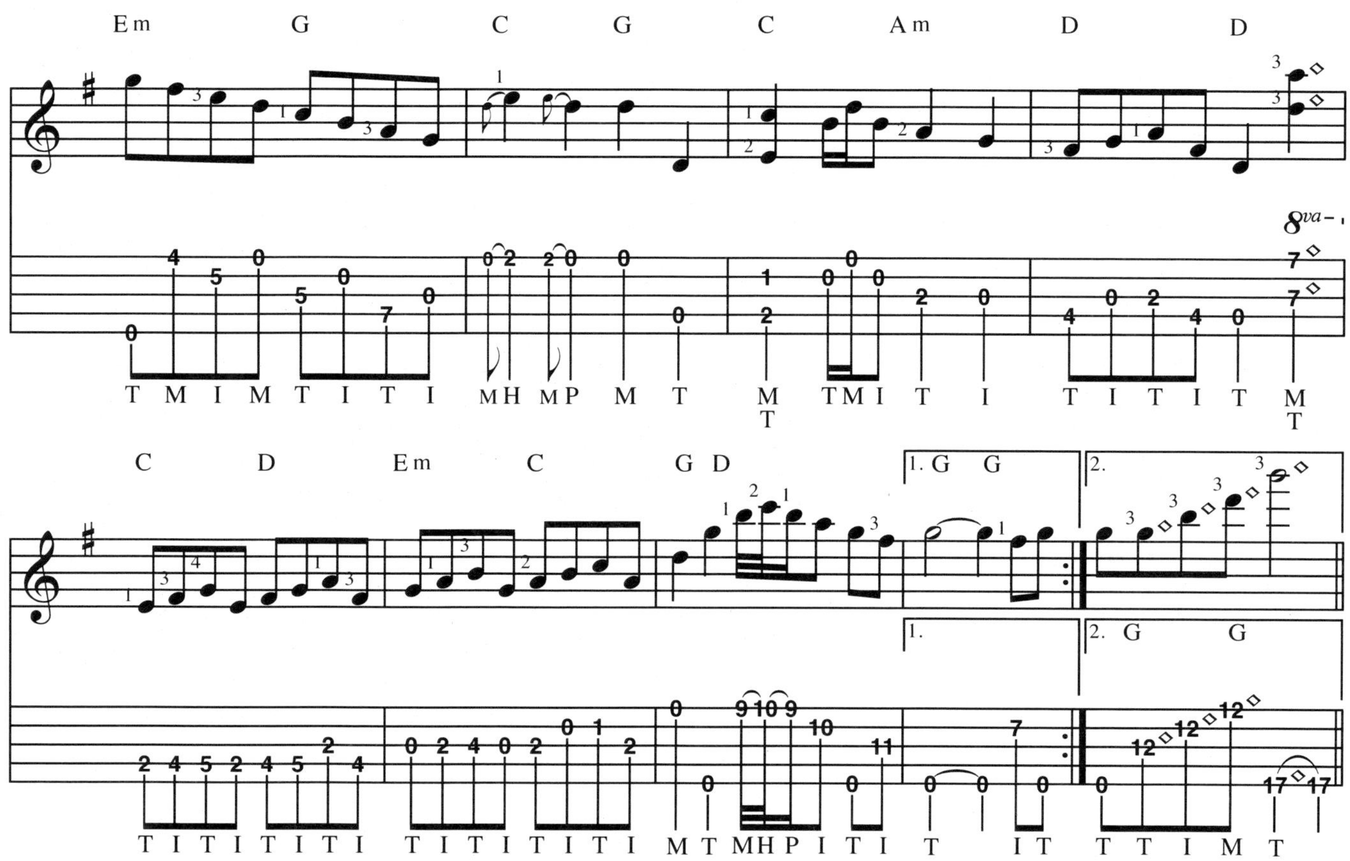
Em G C G C Am D D
T M I M T I T I MH MP M T M T TMI T I T I T I T M T
C D Em C G D 1. G G 2.
1. 2. G G
T I T I T I T I T I T I T I T I M T MHP I T I T I T T T I M T

CAROLAN

Carolan's Dream

Composed by T. or W. Connellan
Adapted by Turlough O'Carolan
Arr. Tom Hanway

♩ = 100

This page has been left blank
to avoid awkward page turns.

Carolan's Ramble to Cashel

♩ = 108

Turlough O'Carolan

Arr. Tom Hanway

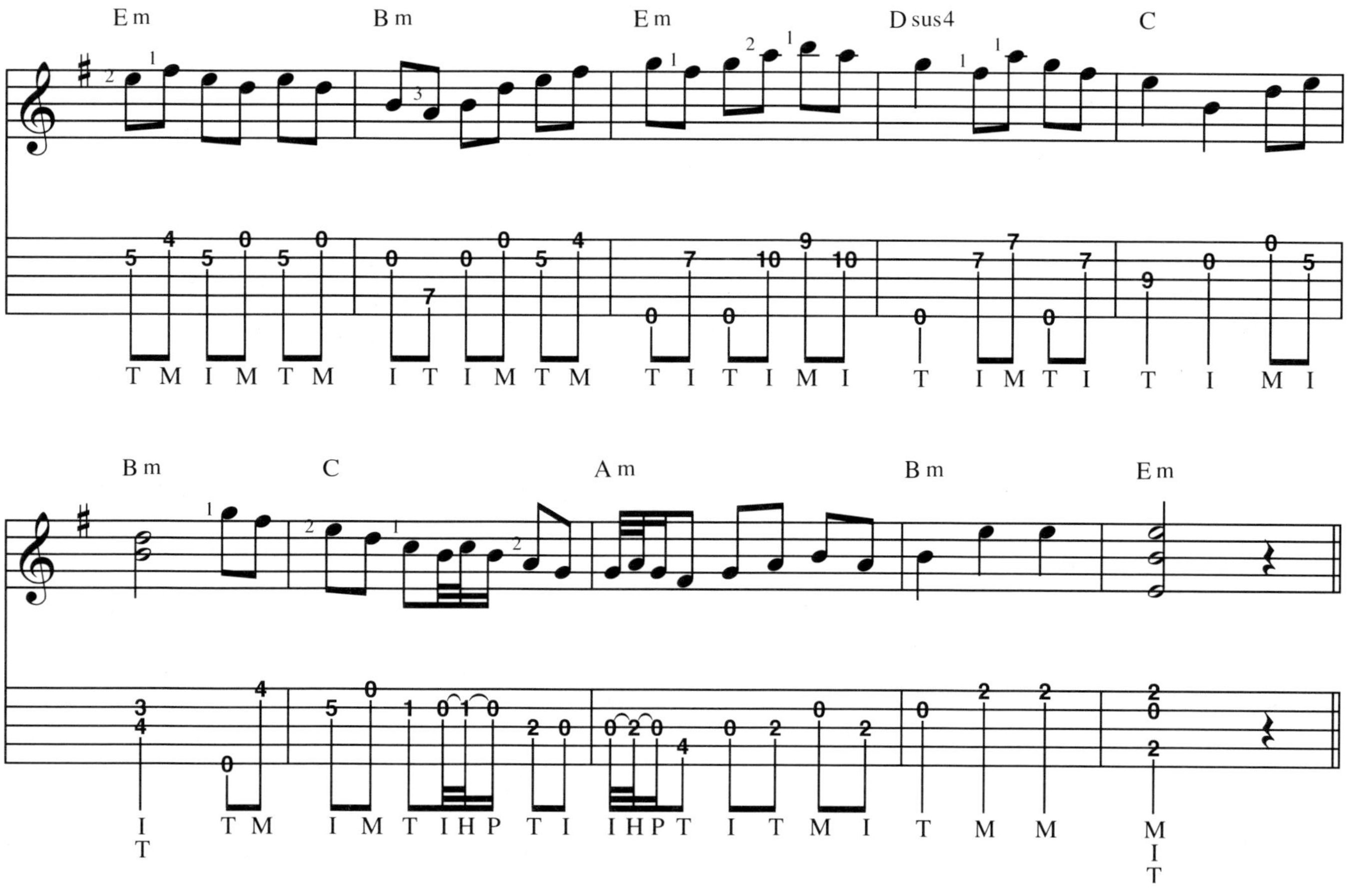
Em
Bm
Em
Dsus4
C
Bm
C
Am
Bm
Em

Carolan's Receipt

(Dr. John Stafford)

♩ = 112

Turlough O'Carolan
Arr. Tom Hanway

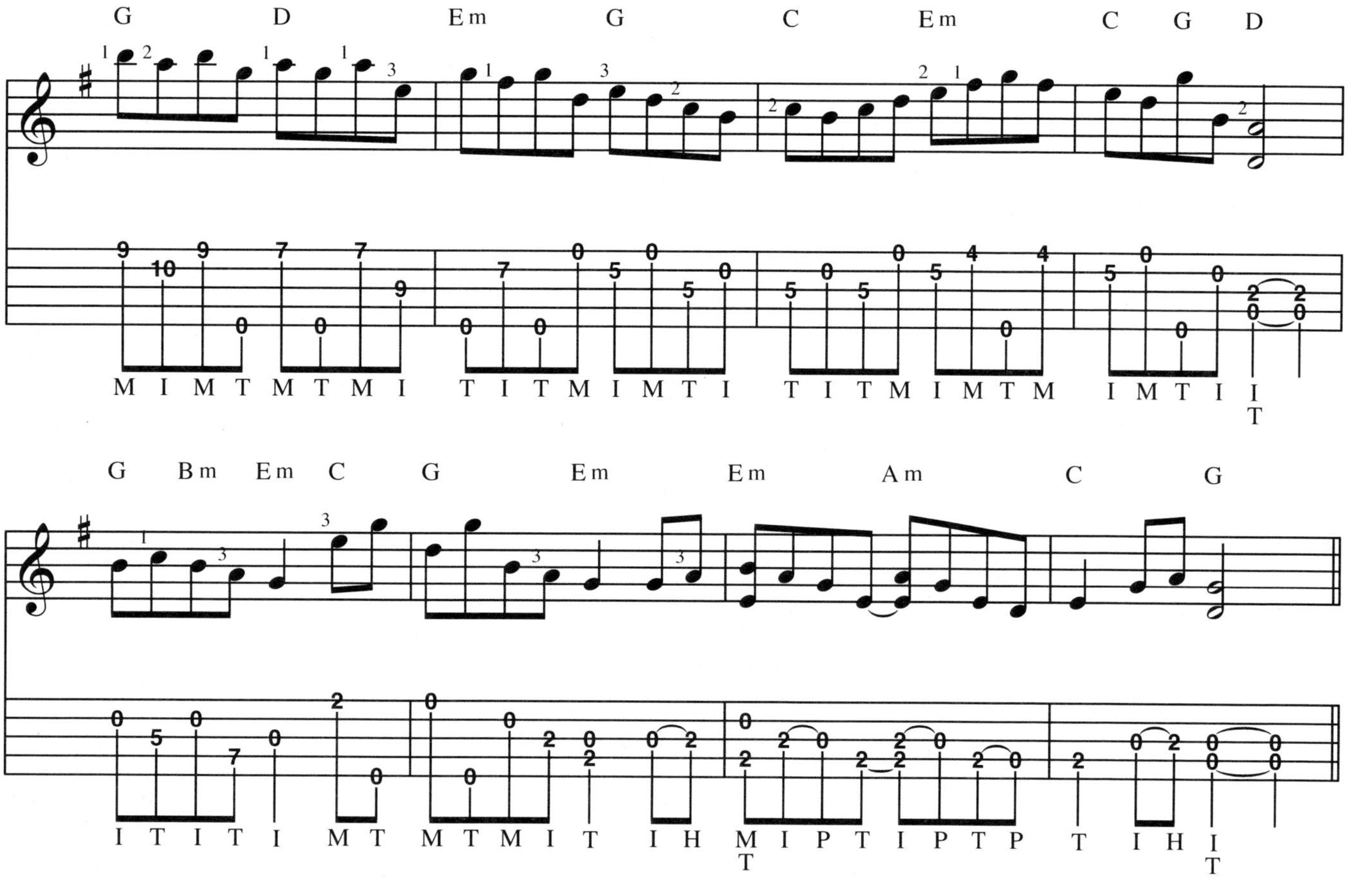
G D Em G C Em C G D
M I M T M T M I T I T M I M T I T I T M I M T M I M T I I T
G Bm Em C G Em Em Am C G
I T I T I M T M T M I T I H M T I P T I P T P T I H I T

♩ = 84

Eleanor Plunkett

In Gratitude to
Noel Sweeney

Turlough O'Carolan
Arr. Tom Hanway

Fanny Power

(Madame Trench)

♩ = 88

Turlough O'Carolan
Arr. Tom Hanway

Henry MacDermott Roe

♩ = 76

Turlough O'Carolan

Arr. Tom Hanway

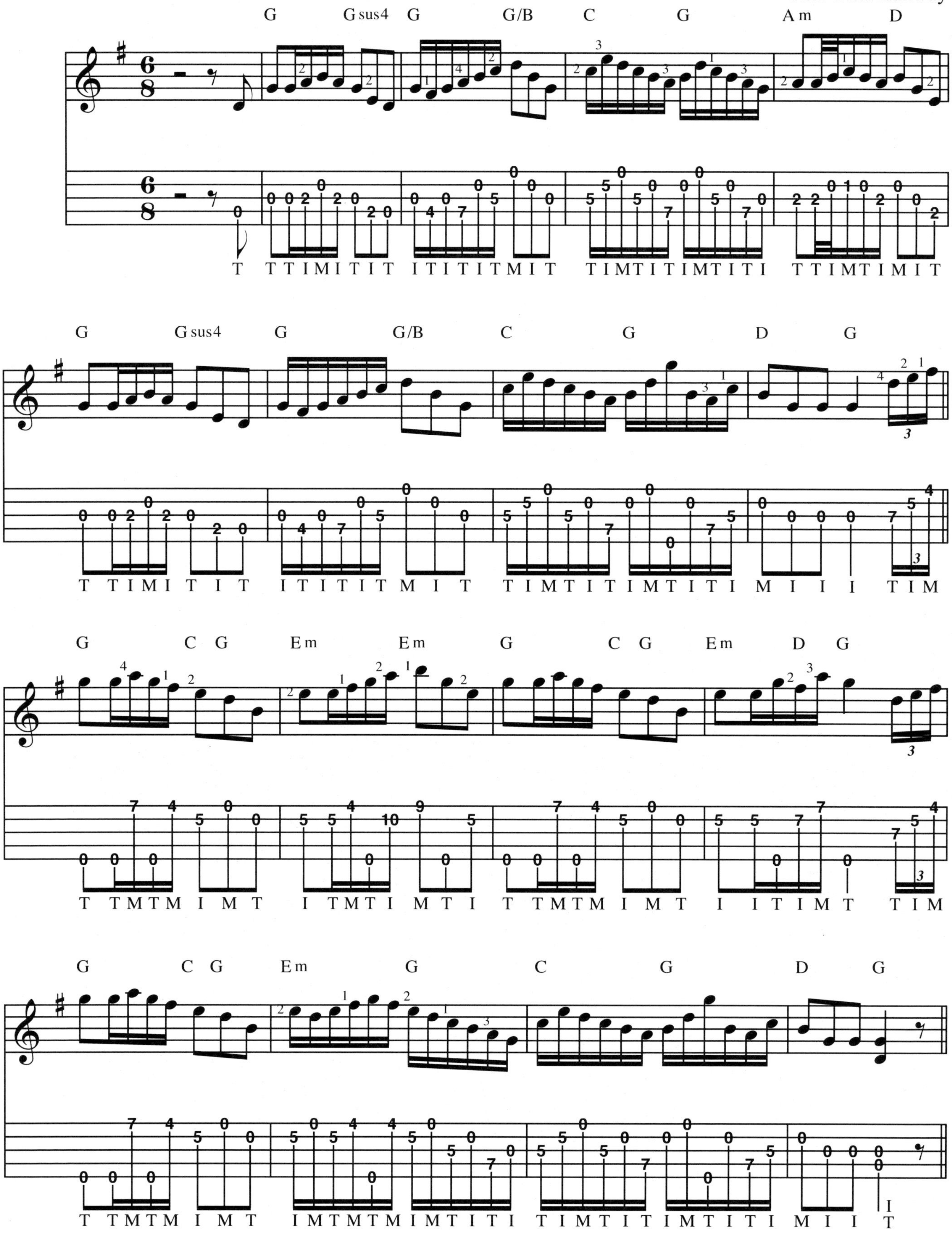

This page has been left blank
to avoid awkward page turns.

Lord Inchiquin

♩ = 160

Turlough O'Carolan

Arr. Tom Hanway

Bm A D G Bm D
Em G6 A A D G
D G Bm D A 1.D 2. D

Morgan Magan

♩ = 144

Turlough O'Carolan
Arr. Tom Hanway

G D Em G C G Am D
I M M I M T T I T M T T I T M I M T I T I
G Bm C G Am G D D
M T M T M I M I M I T I M I T I T T I
C C C C D D D D
T M M I T M M I T M M T I T I T I T I T
G C Am D G D G G
M T M T I M T I T I T I T I T T I T I T I T M T I T

Planxty George Brabazon

(Second Air)

Turlough O'Carolan
Arr. Tom Hanway

♩ = 120

This page has been left blank
to avoid awkward page turns.

Planxty Hugh O'Donnell

♪ = 264

Turlough O'Carolan
Arr. Tom Hanway

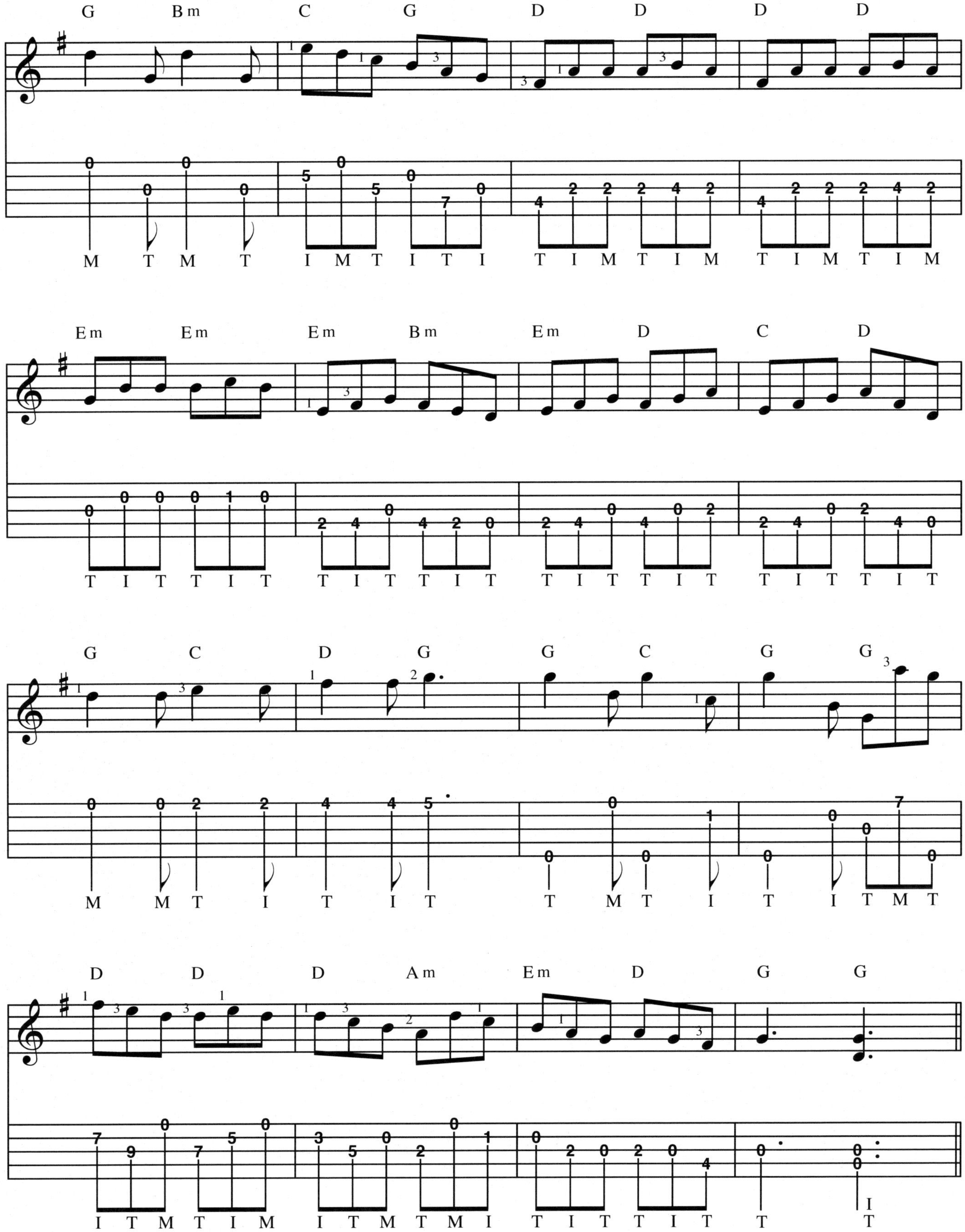
G Bm C G D D D D
M T M T I M T I T I T I M T I M T I M T I M T I M
Em Em Em Bm Em D C D
T I T T I T T I T T I T T I T T I T T I T T I T
G C D G G C G G
M M T I T I T T M T I T I T M T
D D D Am Em D G G
I T M T I M I T M T M I T I T T I T T I T

Planxty Irwin

(Colonel John Irwin)

♩ = 174

Turlough O'Carolan
Arr. Tom Hanway

The Princess Royal

(Miss MacDermott)

♩ = 132

Turlough O'Carolan
Arr. Tom Hanway

♩ = 152

Sheebeg and Sheemore

In gratitude to
Paddy Kiernan

(Sí Bheag, Sí Mhór / The Bonny Cuckoo)

Turlough O'Carolan
Arr. Tom Hanway

Notes on the Tunes

1. Beauty in Tears (related to Llwyn Onn or The Ash Grove)

This tune is attributed to "O'Carolan" in **O'Neill's Music of Ireland (The 1850)**, (Chicago: Lyon & Healy, 1903), No. 635; however, it is not included in the virtually definitive **Donal O'Sullivan** collection, **Carolan: The Life, Times and Music of an Irish Harper,** (Cork: Ossian Publications, 2001 edition). It happens to be an old Welsh folk song, even while it is considered a Carolan tune in Irish circles and played as one. It has many accepted variants, goes by many titles, and is played by folk musicians far and wide, and because it works so well on 5-string banjo it deserves a place in this collection.

Notice the chord arpeggios, ringing open and fretted notes, and chord pinches which emulate the legato style of harping. For rhythmic variation one can also roll the notes in the chords instead of plucking them simultaneously, using either forward or backward roll patterns.

2. Blind Mary

An air and planxty attributed to Carolan (O'Sullivan, No. 182) but without incontrovertible proof. He might have composed it for blind fellow harper and teacher, Máire Dhall (Blind Mary), one of the few women in the harping profession and whom he presumably knew. It can be played slower than I've recorded it here, or even faster, but keep it relaxed and don't rush the ornaments. [O'Sullivan, op, cit. n. 1, 205.]

Notice the *appoggiatura* and *mordent* combination in the second full measure performed by a hammer-on-pull-off combination with the fretting hand. The reason the first two notes (B and C) are not written as *acciaccatura* or grace notes is because I don't play them that quickly, and they subtract time from the principal note (B) that comes last. Appoggiatura can either be ascending or descending to a principal note, or ascending-descending as is the case here. I also use a descending appoggiatura twice in both sections, each time pulling off from an F# to an E-note, an interval of a major second. I like the way these ornaments feel under my fingers, also the way they sound in combination, giving the tune a more Baroque quality.

3. Bridget Cruise (Third Air)

This lovely air or lament is one of many planxties composed for Bridget Cruise, who inspired Carolan to compose many tunes in her honour. It is in 3/4 time, a listening piece, and predates the waltz and mazurka, two popular dance forms originating in continental Europe.

4. Captain O'Kane (The Wounded Hussar)

This tune appears in the O'Sullivan collection (No. 133) on the good authority of previous tune collectors, but with a curious note, "None of the above sources attributes this air to Carolan, but its style resembles his." [O'Sullivan, op, cit. n. 1, 271.] O'Sullivan shares it in E Aeolian, and here is contemporary rendition (B Aeolian). Try to get the most resonance by adhering to the suggested fretting-hand fingerings and holding down strings as long as possible. This produces a more *legato* tone from the banjo. Banjo or violin mutes (or metal tie clips) may also be used if one is so inclined. The second part is repeated in many versions, but I prefer to have the two parts balanced in length.

5. Carolan's Concerto (Mrs. Power)

This is a planxty alternatively known as 'Mrs. Power' (O'Sullivan collection, No. 154). It's more popularly known as 'Carolan's Concerto'. O'Sullivan's older setting, perhaps closer to what Carolan played, or more historically accurate, is not the contemporary norm, and players tend to play a version that is closer to the O'Neill setting ('O'Carolan's Concerto', No. 633) [O'Neill's, op, cit. n. 1, 113.]

My version adds considerable embellishment and rhythmic variation to the latter, and I have arranged it to get good resonance and overtones from the banjo. This is one of Carolan's most cherished and defining works. It works beautifully on 5-string banjo in the original key of D Major. I like to take this one at a brisk tempo but not too quick *(Allegro ma non troppo)*. It makes for an exquisite holiday tune with a glass of sherry.

6. Carolan's Cottage

This melancholic minor tune (A Aeolian) is played by many in E Aeolian, though I prefer the original key (O'Sullivan, No. 184) for 5-string banjo. Donal O'Sullivan notes that this tune's structure is similar to that of 'Lament for Terence MacDonough' (No. 210), an elegy for one of "the most distinguished and versatile Irishmen of his day – a soldier, lawyer, man of affairs poet, and patron of poets…." [O'Sullivan, op, cit. n. 1, 206, 289, 300.]

I like to give this a ringing, mournful quality by placing a metallic mute on the bridge in order to make the banjo resemble the sound of the Gaelic harp (cláirseach) of Carolan's day. Let the chord arpeggios ring, and keep the attack light.

7. Carolan's Draught

This stately air is sometimes played in D Major, and it fits perfectly on the G-tuned 5-string banjo in G Major. Notice the *legato* techniques and fretting-hand fingerings in the first and second parts, particularly the contrary motion in the second full measure. *Staccato* (single-string) techniques are sometimes used, especially towards the end of the second part. This air works beautifully as a seasonal melody along with 'Carolan's Concerto' and so many others composed by the eminent harper.

Legato technique is called "melodic style" in bluegrass and "arpa (harp) style" in classical banjo. It produces a very smooth sound, and differs markedly from "single-string" style, which produces a clipped *staccato* sound. In single-string playing, two or more notes are played on a single string in succession. These fretted notes immediately stop ringing as soon as a blocking finger is lifted or another finger comes down, and this produces the *staccato* effect. I freely mix *legato* and *staccato* techniques within a musical passage if it serves the flow of the tune and sounds good to my ear. The hammer-ons and pull-off patterns mixed with the pedal pitch (a B note) found in the second part use handy fretting- and picking-hand techniques that help to produce a *legato* effect, techniques familiar to classical guitarists.

8. Carolan's Dream (Molly MacAlpin) / Thomas or William Connellan

This beautiful lament, adapted by Carolan from Connellan's 'Molly MacAlpin', has branched out as a tune form and goes under many titles including 'Maud O'Dowd', 'Moll Halfpenny', 'Brian the Brave', and 'Hawke's Hornpipe'. Another is erroneously named 'O'Carolan's Farewell to Music' (No. 700). [O'Neill's, op, cit. n. 1, 129.] This venerable standard (by whichever title) can be played at a slower or faster tempo than I have recorded it here, depending on one's mood or the playing context.

One revealing story is that Carolan "was heard to say that he would rather have been the author of 'Molly MacAlpin' [the original name of the tune] than of any melody he himself had ever composed." [From Edward Bunting, quoted in O'Sullivan, op, cit. n. 1, 289.]

9. Carolan's Ramble to Cashel

This is a very satisfying tune to play in Celtic fingerstyle, but which version to use? The O'Sullivan setting (No. 191) has four odd measures in the third section (measures 9-12) which sound like musical meandering, at least to my ears. I have ignored them in order to keep a more natural-sounding flow in the third section (now 10 measures long). I have also added melismatic-rhythmic ornamentation by using hammer-ons and pull-offs in the fretting-hand – techniques I discuss in detail in Chapter Two of my second collection, **Easy Irish and Celtic Tunes for 5-String Banjo: Best-Loved Jigs and Reels** (Pacific, MO: Mel Bay Publications, Inc., 2012). I like to improvise with the chords, fleshing out the melody as I hear it. More conservative chords and harmonies are, of course, possible.

Many versions combine the second and third parts (as a B Part) and repeat them to make 36 measures (not including the first part). I much prefer 18 bars (eight plus ten) to follow the first part (eight bars repeated or 16 measures). The tune sounds more balanced this way. Be careful not to rush this tune. Let it ring, and really feel its contours under your fingers. [O'Sullivan, op, cit. n. 1, 209, 291.]

10. Carolan's Receipt (Dr. John Stafford)

Some amusing drinking stories (true or exaggerations of more-or-less true stories) are connected to this lively melody, a planxty written by Carolan at the house of his life-long friend, Dr. John Stafford of Portabello, near Elphin, County Roscommon. The doctor attended to Carolan during his final illness and helped bear the harper's coffin at his funeral. Put energy into this tune and really feel it, with or without a dram of whiskey.

11. Eleanor Plunkett

This is a very touching melody. I may play it a bit faster than most harpers or harpists would because it feels right that way on the 5-string. I also enjoy using a lot of arpeggios played with either a forward roll or thumb-stroke, which are virtually interchangeable; however, the thumb-stroke is louder and gutsier, while the forward roll is more subtle and requires more restraint. Sometimes I prefer to rake across the strings with my thumb because it feels more comfortable and is less fussy. Also notice the voice-leading (melody on top) and walking bass in the second part.

Carolan wrote four verses in praise of Eleanor Plunkett of Robertstown, Co. Meath, who was the only survivor of her family. One story, impossible to verify in its details, relates that 30 members of her family shut themselves inside Castlecome, a castle two miles from Robertstown, "which was destroyed by boiling water." [O'Sullivan, op, cit. n. 1, 181, 279.]

12. Fanny Power (Madame Trench)

Fanny (Frances) Power was the daughter and heiress of David and Elizabeth Power of Coorheen, Loughrea. It must have been written before her marriage to Richard Trench "because in the second verse Carolan expresses the hope that he will live to dance at her wedding." [O'Sullivan, op, cit. n. 1, 181, 280-281.]

Play this one gently and let the notes ring for as long as possible. Folks like to argue about whether it's a jig or a waltz. It's a Carolan tune, predating the waltz form, and in 6/8 tune. Of course, it can be slowed down to make for a waltz; or alternatively, it can be sped up and played almost as a jig, even combined with jigs. It's fine on its own.

13. Henry MacDermott Roe (First Air)

Here is another delightful tune to play, as if Turlough O'Carolan composed it for the benefit of 5-string banjo players. Although the time signature indicates 6/8, this tune is not a jig. It could be re-written in 3/4 time, but that doesn't make it a waltz, per se. It can also be written in 6/4 time. I've stuck to the original length and 6/8 time signature; however, I've added my own chords. Can it be given a waltz treatment? Yes, one can find it listed as a waltz in places such as The Session on-line. Many Carolan tunes (in 6/8, 6/4 or 3/4) could also be given some kind of "waltz" treatment, but it's important to remember that they all predate and were not influenced by the Continental waltz.

Celtic fingerstyle constantly makes use of variation and ornamentation, mixing legato and staccato fingerings, and this is explained for fully in **Easy Irish and Celtic Tunes for 5-String Banjo: Best-Loved Jigs and Reels** [Hanway, op, cit. n. 9, Chapter One: Variation and Ornamentation, 9-11, 162, 168-169.] That collection also summarizes the three main types of Celtic variation. An in-depth comparison between the three types of Celtic variation with concrete tune examples can also be found in the **Complete Book of Irish & Celtic 5-String Banjo** (Pacific, MO: Mel Bay Publications, Inc., 1998), which has a cross-referenced Glossary and 101 tunes transcribed.

Donal O'Sullivan points out, "The MacDermott Roe family of Alderford were Carolan's principal patrons and oldest friends, and some account of them is given in Part One (Chapter 5)." [O'Sullivan, op, cit. n. 1, 252.]

14. Lord Inchiquin

Another satisfying tune to play in Celtic fingerstyle, pay close attention to the contrary motion and fretting-hand fingerings in the fourth and fifth measures, also the use of fretting-hand ornamentation in the form of hammer-ons and pull-offs. I could have made this tune a bit simpler, but it's more satisfying to work in bass lines, interval pinches and Baroque ornaments. I could have decorated a lot more than is shown here. Have fun with it and add your own decorations to it.

O'Sullivan notes, "The subject is doubtless the 4th Earl of Inchiquin, who succeeded to the title on his father's death, 24th December 1719, and died in 1777. The family seat was (and is) in Dromoland Castle, Newmarket-on-Fergus, County Clare, which is not far from Doonass, where Carolan visited Rev. Charles Massey.... It is probable that this piece is composed on that occasion." [O'Sullivan, op, cit. n. 1, 245.]

15. Morgan Magan

In many older versions the parts are doubled, as in the O'Sullivan setting (No. 92). I find the tune a bit ponderous if played that way, so I have halved the parts, and it can be played several times this way without seeming too long. "Vivace" is indicated for tempo, which I have chosen to play at 144 beats per minute to keep the tune stately. If the tempo is too slow the tune seems to wither; meanwhile, if played too fast the melody isn't given a chance to come into flower. I prefer a slightly more *staccato* approach for this one, and use fretting-hand fingerings that feel good to me. One can find other *legato* ways of playing this, even getting more of an open ring out of the banjo. Still, there are plenty of open strings, lots of overtones and pleasing *partials* happening throughout the tune.

This is yet another planxty, and writes O'Sullivan, "This lively tune was composed by Carolan in honour of Morgan Magan of Togherstown, County Westmeath, who died in 1738. He was a younger son of Morgan Magan of Cloney, in the same county, and his sister Susanna married Sir Arthur Shaen, who is the subject of no. 159." [O'Sullivan, op, cit. n. 1, 150, 258.]

16. Planxty George Brabazon (Second Air)

This tune in its original key lends itself beautifully to G-tuned banjo. Be careful not to rush this one. I like it no faster than 120 beats per minute, and it sounds lovely played as a slow air, adding rubato. I have kept the tempo steady here, as for all the tunes, but most of these can be played with varying degrees of *rubato.*

O'Sullivan includes this (No. 7) and notes, "This air makes its sole appearance in the section of Captain *O'Neill's Music of Ireland* (1903) devoted to Carolan's compositions. As I have been unable to trace whence he obtained it, I mark it as doubtful, but it resembles Carolan in style and it may well have been written by him." [O'Sullivan, op, cit. n. 1, 107, 228.]

17. Planxty Hugh O'Donnell

This air was composed for Hugh O'Donnell (No. 127) of Newport, County Mayo, who was son of Colonel Manus O'Donnell, according to O'Sullivan. Hugh Roe O'Donnell (30 October 1572 – 10 September 1602) or Red Hugh O'Donnell (Aodh Ruadh Ó Domhnaill) left a huge legacy for his heroic deeds and oratorical prowess. He was Rí (king) of *Dun na nGall* (Donegal). He is sometimes also known as Aodh Ruadh II or Red Hugh II, being the son of Aodh mac Maghnusa Ó Domhnaill (Sir Hugh O'Donnell), King of *Tír Chonaill* (Tyrconnell or modern Donegal), who abdicated the thrown for his son. (He died around 1600.) With the aid of Hugh O'Neill, Red Hugh O'Donnell led a rebellion against English government in Ireland from 1593 and helped to lead the Nine Years' War (against English occupation) from 1595 to 1603.

My wife Denise traces her ancestry back to these same O'Donnell's, and ultimately to Hugh Roe O'Donnell's family through her grandmother, Alice O'Donnell. My first wife, Kathleen Hanway (nee Low), whom I lost to cancer, comes from Donnelly stock, tracing her ancestry back to these same O'Donnells. I first learned about Red Hugh O'Donnell through her, connecting her ancestors to the legendary O'Donnell clan. So, it is an honour to include this venerable tune here for my dear departed Kathleen and my present love Denise.

This tune is played many different ways and in various keys. Notice that it is in 6/8 and makes for a jig. Slowed down considerably, it can be used as a set dance; however, its length could be at issue: Is it too long? I have kept it to the length (32 measures) as O'Sullivan has it, though many versions double the parts, or just the first part. It works perfectly on the 5-string banjo in the key of G. (O'Sullivan has it in C.) Many of Carolan's planxties sound like ancient jigs, but this one is truly a regal melody. [O'Sullivan, op, cit. n. 1, 169, 269.]

18. Planxty Irwin (Colonel John Irwin)

I have a less decorated version of this in **Complete Book of Irish & Celtic 5-String Banjo** (1998). Here I add more ornaments, leaning into principal melody notes using chord *arpeggios.* This gives the tune a more

Baroque feel. I use harmony notes as in my earlier setting; however, chords are indicated here to help tune backers, as for all the tunes.

O'Sullivan has this in 6/8 time and in C Major (No. 59), with no repeats for either section. I prefer to double the parts, as others have done, making it a 32-bar instead of a 16-bar tune. [Hanway, op, cit. n. 13, 41; O'Sullivan, op, cit. n. 1, 133.]

19. Princess Royal, The (Miss MacDermott)

This natural minor melody has an exotic Middle Eastern ring to it. Sullivan has it F minor (No. 87), and it is popular in E minor. I have chosen G minor in order to play drone notes, especially a low D note (open fourth string), also for the challenge of playing in G natural minor without retuning the banjo. Only the open B-string does not work (open) for this tune, though I fret it a lot in order to get main melody notes. Notice the contrary motion and arpeggios which give the tune a Baroque quality.

Many versions double both parts, but I have kept it the same length as O'Sullivan, who observes, "'The Princess Royal' is one of the most celebrated of Carolan's compositions, largely because of its association with the words of the song 'The Arethusa', to which it was set by Shield towards the end of the eighteenth century." [O'Sullivan, op, cit. n. 1, 148, 254.]

20. Sheebeg and Sheemore (Sí Bheag, Sí Mhór / related to The Bonny Cuckoo)

Another version of this, titled 'Sí Bheag Agus Sí Mhór', played an octave higher with a raised fifth string, is found in my **Complete Book of Irish & Celtic 5-String Banjo**. Here I have kept it to standard G tuning, adding chord *arpeggios* in both parts, and a *trill* in the second part. Sometimes I leave out the trill and play a slightly simpler *appoggiatura* and *mordent* combination, a single hammer-on-pull-off combination. O'Sullivan version (No. 202) indicates trills in four different spots. I find this a bit busy on the 5-string and use simpler ornaments, including *harmonics* to get more ring from the banjo.

Also, I have further adapted this tune using intervallic variation, raising the low notes so that the melody may be more easily sung (key of G). A new wassailing song has emerged out of this, 'The Apple Tree', which has three verses collected and penned by friend and author Judy Harrow. Because it has lyrics, and Judy (now deceased) wanted to keep it copyright-free, it's best not to include it here, but I will record it. I also plan to put a video online – a sung version of 'The Apple Tree' in the key of G – when the time is right.

Judy wrote this about the origins of the lyrics to 'The Apple Tree': It was mid-November, 1990. We had been at a spiritual retreat weekend at a Quaker facility in the Berkshire Mountains of Massachusetts, a centuries-old farmhouse with a large, beautiful, ancient, apple tree growing near the door. Only the few of us who had that Monday off work stayed for the last night, with nothing to do but relax and enjoy each other's company.

Tom was just learning to play 'Sí Bheag, Sí Mhór' on his guitar. He played it over and over to "get it into his fingers." The words seemed to emerge from Carolan's music and from the whole group. I was really only the scribe. I suspect the inspiration was actually a gift from the lovely old tree just outside our door. [Hanway, op, cit. n. 13, 136; O'Sullivan, op, cit. n. 1, 214.]

Bibliography

Clarke, H.P. *The New Approach to Uilleann Piping.* Cork, Ireland: Ossian Publications, 1998.
Cooper, Peter. *Mel Bay's Complete Irish Fiddle Player.* Pacific, MO: Mel Bay Publications, Inc., 1995.

Cranitch, Matt. *The Irish Fiddle Book.* Cork, Ireland: Ossian Publications, 2001. First published 1988 by The Mercier Press.

Hanway, Tom. *Complete Book of Irish & Celtic 5-String Banjo.* Pacific, MO: Mel Bay Publications, Inc., 1998.

Hanway, Tom. *Easy Irish and Celtic Melodies for 5-String Banjo: Best-Loved Airs and Session Tunes.* Pacific, MO: Mel Bay Publications, Inc., 2013.

Hanway, Tom. *Easy Irish and Celtic Session Tunes for 5-String Banjo: Best-Loved Jigs and Reels.* Pacific, MO: Mel Bay Publications, Inc., 2012.

Grossman, Stefan, Duck Baker, and El McMeen. *Mel Bay's Complete Celtic Fingerstyle Guitar.* Pacific, MO: Mel Bay Publications, Inc., 1995.

Grossman, Stefan and John Renbourn. *Mel Bay's Deluxe Anthology of O'Carolan Music.* Pacific, MO: Mel Bay Publications, Inc., 1995.

Loughnane, Kathleen. *The Harpers Connellan: Irish Music of the Late 17th Century.* Galway, Ireland: Reiskmore Music, 2009.

McQuaid, Sarah. *The Irish DADGAD Guitar Book: Playing and Backing Traditional Irish Music on Open-Tune Guitar.* Cork, Ireland: Ossian Publications, 1995.

Nelson, Mark. *Complete Book of Celtic Music for Appalachian Dulcimer.* Pacific, MO: Mel Bay Publications, Inc., 1995.

Ó Canainn, Tómas. *Traditional Slow Airs of Ireland.* Cork, Ireland: Ossian Publications, 1995.

O'Neill, Capt. Francis. *O'Neill's Music of Ireland.* Pacific, MO: Mel Bay Publications, Inc., 1996. First published 1903 by Lyon & Healy.

O'Neill, Capt. Francis. *Waifs and Strays of Gaelic Melody.*, reprinted, Dublin: The Mercier Press, 1980.

O'Riada, Seán. *Our Musical Heritage.* Mountrath, Co. Laois: The Dolmen Press, 1982.

O'Sullivan, Donal. Carolan: *The Life, Times and Music of an Irish Harper.* Cork, Ireland: Ossian Publications, 2001. First published1958 by Routledge and Paul.

Smith, Chris. *Celtic Back-Up for all Instrumentalists.* Pacific, MO: Mel Bay Publications, Inc., 1999.

Williamson, Robin. *English, Welsh, Scottish & Irish Fiddle Tunes.* New York, NY: Oak Publications, 1976.

Credits

Front Cover:

Carolan and Hanway Having the Craic, Mohill, Co. Leitrim (Photo: Denise Conroy)

Art and Photos:

Back Cover:

Carolan and Hanway Play Carolan's Draught, Mohill, Co. Leitrim (Photo: Denise Conroy)

Tune Index with Tempos

Play-along, up-to-speed tempos for the online audio recording are indicated below:

For most tunes: ♩ = beats per minute (bpm).

For some tunes: ♪ = beats per minute (bpm).

The Author

Carolan, Hanway and Mr. Hunter in Mohill

Tom Hanway is an American 5-string banjoist, guitarist and composer. He wears many musical hats, produces and does studio session work on both sides of the Atlantic. Tom learned to play the banjo in the 1980s, studying with Tony Trischka and Bill Keith, also being inspired by the playing of Earl Scruggs, Don Reno, J.D. Crowe, Jerry Garcia, Béla Fleck, and Vassar Clements. In the late 80s and early 90s he worked with the John Herald Band (former Greenbriar Boys), Blue Horizon, Burnt Toast, and with Kenny Kosek in the off-Broadway bluegrass musical ***Feast Here Tonight***. Hanway has also performed in concert with Bill Monroe, Peter Rowan, Vassar Clements, Rick Danko and Levon Helm. He was co-promoter with Kathleen Low Hanway (1960-2002) of the Big Apple Bluegrass & Folk Festival in New York City (1997-2002).

Since the publication of his seminal work (100 tunes) in 1998, ***Complete Book of Irish & Celtic 5-String Banjo*** (MB 95759 BCD), Hanway has pioneered "Celtic fingerstyle banjo." ***Bluegrass Unlimited*** wrote in January 1999: "What Earl Scruggs' book did for bluegrass banjo, Tom Hanway's book may well do for the 5-string in Irish and Celtic music, and will certainly become regarded as **'the bible'** for any 5-string player with an interest in this joyous music." This is a Mel Bay best-seller and has won Tom many converts on both sides of the Atlantic. In 2012 Hanway followed up with ***Easy Irish and Celtic Session Tunes for 5-String Banjo: Best Loved Jigs and Reels,*** transcribing and recording 68 tunes. His third collection, **Easy Irish and Celtic**

Melodies for 5-String Banjo: Best-Loved Airs and Session Tunes includes 32 more airs, songs and melodies. Tom's fourth collection, 20 O'Carolan Irish Classics for 5-String Banjo and All Instruments (MB 21599 BCD) presents 20 best-loved, timeless harp tunes by the eminent Irish composer and lyricist.

Tom is a fan of traditional music from all over the world and enjoys working with different artists. He has played on dozens of recordings on both sides of the Atlantic and has produced three recordings on the Joyous Gard Records label. For his debut CD, **Bucket of Bees** (1991), Tom enlisted bluegrass luminaries Sam Bush, Jerry Douglas, Stuart Duncan, Vassar Clements, David Grier, Bill Keith, Mark Schatz, and Tony Trischka. Recorded in Nashville and New York City, this groundbreaking CD got rave reviews and a full-page "Highlight" review in ***Bluegrass Unlimited*** magazine. Hanway's 'Elephant Hop' was chosen for **KBC's Prime Cuts of Bluegrass, Volume 1**, and in a Nationwide Poll was voted "No. 1" by America's top bluegrass deejays, Tom's original tune edging out a powerhouse duet ('Carolina Traveler') recorded by banjoists Earl Scruggs and John McEuen. **Bucket of Bees** features seven original instrumentals and incorporates bluegrass, newgrass, Celtic and jazz. **Tom Hanway & Blue Horizon** further reveals Tom's skills as a tunesmith, arranger and producer. Hanway (alias "Badbelly") also sings traditional country blues and gospel songs, fingerpicking guitar and 5-string banjo. Renowned fiddler Vassar Clements (1928-2005) joins him on his tour de force blues-guitar project: **The Badbelly Project: Hesitation Blues**. Vassar Clements plays on all of Hanway's Joyous Gard recordings.

In 1997 Hanway teamed up with banjo manufacturer Geoff Stelling to co-design the **Stelling SwallowTail Deluxe** and **Standard** banjo, a production model instrument. The **SwallowTail** has become a popular model for Stelling, used for bluegrass, Celtic and other styles of music, with actor Steve Martin purchasing one true to Tom's original model.

Tom Hanway is a musical shape-shifter, a veteran of many styles of music who feels blessed to be working in life with other like-minded artists at something that he loves. He regularly travels back and forth between Ireland and the United States playing and collecting tunes.

Discography

Bucket of Bees (Joyous Gard Records, 1991)
Tom Hanway & Blue Horizon (Joyous Gard Records, 1992)
Burnt Toast (Joyous Gard Records, 1996)
Complete Book of Irish & Celtic 5-String Banjo (Mel Bay Publications, Inc., 1998)
Grillbillies Album, Volumes 1 and 2 (Yee Haw Records, 1999)
The Badbelly Project: Hesitation Blues (Joyous Gard Records, 2005)
Easy Irish and Celtic Session Tunes for 5-String Banjo: Best-Loved Jigs and Reels (Mel Bay Publications, Inc., 2012)
Easy Irish and Celtic Melodies for 5-String Banjo: Best-Loved Jigs and Reels (Mel Bay Publication, Inc., 2013)
The Carnival Brothers: 'The Sun is Gonna Shine' – pop single (Fret Sounds: 2013)
The Carnival Brothers: 'Carnival Station' – pop single (Fret Sounds: 2014)

Official Website: www.tomhanway.com

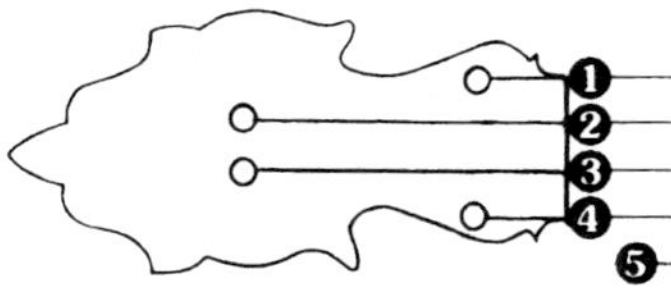

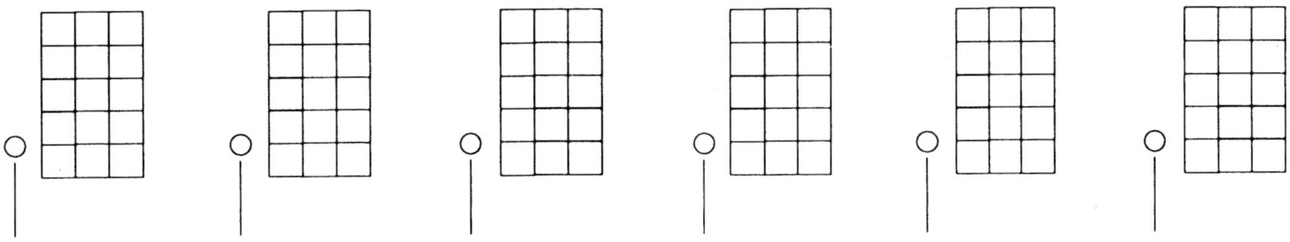

WWW.MELBAY.COM